S0-FLQ-125

HOW TO BE A GROWING CHRISTIAN

A BASIC GUIDE TO DISCIPLESHIP

Bennie E. Goodwin II

INTERVARSITY PRESS
DOWNERS GROVE, ILLINOIS 60515

©1987 by Bennie E. Goodwin II

All rights reserved. No part of this book may be reproduced in any form without written permission from InterVarsity Press, P.O. Box 1400, Downers Grove, Illinois 60515.

InterVarsity Press is the book-publishing division of InterVarsity Christian Fellowship, a student movement active on campus at hundreds of universities, colleges and schools of nursing. For information about local and regional activities, write Public Relations Dept., InterVarsity Christian Fellowship, 6400 Schroeder Rd., P.O. Box 7895, Madison, WI 53707-7895.

Distributed in Canada through InterVarsity Press, 860 Denison St., Unit 3, Markham, Ontario L3R 4H1, Canada.

All Scripture quotations, unless otherwise indicated, are from The Revised Standard Version of the Bible, copyrighted 1946, 1952, 1971 by the Division of Christian Education of the National Council of the Churches of Christ in the USA, and are used by permission. All rights reserved.

ISBN 0-87784-573-5

Printed in the United States of America

Library of Congress Cataloging in Publication Data

Goodwin, Bennie E., 1933-
     How to be a growing Christian.

     Bibliography: p.
     1. Christian life—1960-   I. Title.
BV4501.2.G625   1987   248.4   86-33737
ISBN 0-87784-573-5 (pbk.)

16	15	14	13	12	11	10	9	8	7	6	5	4	3	2
99	98	97	96	95	94	93	92	91	90	89				

1 Growing Up Is Hard to Do	*7*
2 What Is Spiritual Growth?	*9*
3 Why Bother? *15*	
4 Building Spiritual Muscles	*23*
5 Developing Day by Day	*33*
6 Faith for the Long Run	*39*
Notes *45*	
Further Reading *47*	

1
GROWING UP IS HARD TO DO

I used to believe that there were a lot of different things going on in and around the Christian life. And in a sense there are a great variety of activities that swirl around Christian people and institutions. But I have come to the conclusion that all the things we do can be put under one of three major categories: salvation, Christian service, and the spiritual growth which connects them.

In this pamphlet I want to concentrate on the subject of spiritual growth. It is the process that enhances the experience of salvation and prepares believers for effective Christian service.

About five centuries before Jesus there lived one of history's most colorful characters. His name was Socrates.[1] He is usually thought of as the father of Western philosophy and the most famous professional philosopher to die for his beliefs. But perhaps he is most well known for his way of teaching. Socrates did not lecture to his students, but engaged them in conversations called dialogs.

It is said that Socrates began his dialogs by asking the question, "What is it?" To have effective dialog, he thought it was important for everyone involved in the conversation to at least agree about or understand what it was that they were all talking about. So he began with a definition of terms.

It is with that attitude that I wish to begin this conversation with you. In chapter one I discuss the question, "What is spiritual growth?" And after a descriptive answer to that question, the rest of the book is devoted to asking and answering three other questions. In chapter two I ask, "Why is spiritual growth necessary?" Chapter three answers the question, "How do we grow spiritually?" and chapter four discusses the question, "How can we remain spiritually strong?"

I have three types of people in mind as I write this pamphlet. First, this is for new Christians who want to grow from spiritual infancy to maturity. Second, it is for Christians who recognize that they have grown spiritually but are seeking help so that they can live a consistently high-quality Christian life. Third, this pamphlet is for persons who are looking for a simple, brief piece of literature on spiritual growth that they can share with others.

If this book fulfills any or all of these purposes, I believe the Lord will be praised, and I will be pleased.

2
WHAT IS SPIRITUAL GROWTH?

We all know what it means to grow. Somewhere in your closet you may have stashed away a chart where your mother or father recorded your height at various times during your childhood. You can look over that chart and see just how tall you were when you were 2 years old and 4 years old and even 15 years old. But what is spiritual growth? How can we chart it? How can we know if we are growing spiritually?

Spiritual growth is difficult to define, but I think it can be summed up in three phrases. First, it is an increasing *awareness* of the presence and power of God. Second, it is the gradual acquiring of spiritual *attributes*. And third, it is an increased *availability* to God. These phrases come alive vividly when seen in the light of the exciting episode recorded in Isaiah 6:1-9:

> In the year that King Uzziah died I saw the Lord sitting upon a throne, high and lifted up; and his train filled the temple. Above him stood the seraphim; each had six wings: with two he covered his face, and with two he covered his feet, and with two he flew. And one called to another and said:
>
> > "Holy, holy, holy is the LORD of hosts; the whole earth is full of his glory."
>
> And the foundations of the thresholds shook at the voice of him who called, and the house was filled with smoke. And I said: "Woe is me! For I am lost; for I am a man of unclean lips, and I dwell in the midst of a people of unclean lips; for my eyes have seen the King, the LORD of hosts!"
>
> Then flew one of the seraphim to me, having in his hand a burning coal which he had taken with tongs from the altar. And he touched my mouth, and said: "Behold, this has touched your lips; your guilt is taken away, and your sin forgiven." And I heard the voice of the Lord saying, "Whom shall I send, and who will go for us?" Then I said, "Here am I! Send me."

This episode took place in the life of a young priest named Isaiah shortly after the death of his hero, King Uzziah. Uzziah had been a good man and an effective administrator. But being overly impressed with his own success, he, as King, decided to take over one of the priest's functions and offer a sacrifice on the temple altar. As he did so he was struck with leprosy (2 Chronicles 26).

When the great King Uzziah died a leper, Isaiah was griefstricken and despondent. How could a king who had served God so nobly and done so much good for so many people, change so drastically, sin so deliberately and be punished so terribly? Isaiah must have been asking many such questions as he made his way to the temple one Sabbath morning.

An Increasing Awareness

But once inside the temple, Isaiah's spirit was lifted from his doubts, despondency and self-pity when he saw the Lord. He saw angels calling to one another. He saw smoke rising from a heavenly altar. He felt the temple pillars move with the power of God. He saw God's royal robes filling earthly space. In the midst of his troubles he became aware of the presence and power of God. He had a spiritual experience.

Our own experiences may not be as dramatic as Isaiah's but they can be just as real. I was standing over the bathroom sink one day washing my socks. I had some rather pressing bills that I didn't have enough money to pay. I was worrying and fretting when I heard the Spirit say quietly, "Bennie, these bills have not taken me by surprise. I am aware of these bills and have already made provision to help you pay them. I have handled them before, haven't I? Do you think you can trust me?" As you might expect, I grew a few inches from that experience.

You see, God is always aware of us. Jesus said that even the hairs on our head are numbered (Luke 12:7). Spiritual growth happens as we become more and more aware of God. Anything, including troubles, trials and temptations, that makes us more aware of God's presence and power may be a source of spiritual growth.

Acquiring Attributes

Another part of Isaiah's experience clarifies for us a further aspect of spiritual development. When Isaiah saw the Lord, he also saw himself and his inadequacy. The new awareness of God's presence and power threw into bold relief Isaiah's own sinfulness. He realized when he heard angel voices that his own speech and the conversation of his friends left much to be desired. He realized he was "undone," incomplete, not together. He realized he had something he didn't want and wanted something he didn't have—holiness.

But when the Lord heard Isaiah's confession, he took his sins away and gave him forgiveness and assurance.

Spiritual growth is characterized by a sense of cleansing and an assurance of being "added to." In the New Testament, Paul calls these new attributes the "fruit of the Spirit" (Galatians 5:22-23). These spiritual qualities really describe the personality of Jesus. He personified love, joy, peace, patience, kindness, goodness, faithfulness, gentleness and self-control. What happens in the process of spiritual growth is that the Spirit takes the qualities of Jesus' personality and adds them to the Christian's personality so that the growing Christian becomes more and more like Jesus.

The way I know I'm growing spiritually is that I am increasingly aware of God's presence and power in my daily life, and I see more and more of Jesus' characteristics in my personality and behavior.

One of the areas in my life where I have noticed the most growth is the area of patience. Several years ago I taught music in junior high school and had one class—all boys—that was especially challenging. As the students were leaving the class one day, a relatively innocent-looking teen-ager walked past me and whispered an obscenity.

We couldn't hit students in those days but before he knew it, he was up in the air and being pushed (by me) against a concrete wall. After I had rubbed him across the wall for a few feet I put him down and let him go to his next class. I really didn't know I had that kind of temper.

Fortunately, I've changed. When a woman insulted me recently with words she knew were not true, not only did I stay cool and calm, but I felt genuine pity for her. I was amazed by this sense of pity. I knew it was not my normal reaction, but a work of the Spirit who had brought about growth in my personality. I know the Lord is not yet finished with me, but there is a certain inner satisfaction in seeing a positive change in my reactions and behaviors.

Growing Availability

The third way that I know I'm growing spiritually is that more and more of me becomes more and more available to God. When Isaiah experienced his tremendous awareness of God and of himself and was assured that his relationship with God was now positive, he heard God ask, "Whom shall I send, and who will go for us?" And Isaiah immediately made himself available.

"Here am I!" he said. "Send me" (6:8).

The measure of our spiritual growth is the extent of our availability to God. God will use children like Little Brother Two Fish (John 6:1-15), young people like David (1 Samuel 17:1-58), and old people like Moses (Exodus 14). He will use sick people like Mr. Legion (Luke 8:22-29), rich people like Lydia (Acts 16:13-15), Black people like Martin Luther King, Jr., and White people like D. L. Moody. He will use Catholic people like Mother Teresa, and Baptist people like Billy Graham. He will use good unbelievers like Cyrus (Ezra 1) and believers with a bad past like Saul of Tarsus (Acts 9). The one major requirement of being used by God is availability.

No matter how lacking we are in talents, knowledge, money or power, if we are available, God will use us beyond our highest expectations. In fact, Paul says that sometimes God deliberately chooses the foolish, weak, base and despised who are available to show his wisdom, strength, power and creativity (1 Corinthians 1:27-31). The reason God can do so much with so little is because what is done is not dependent on the resource but the Source. The fact that Little Brother Two Fish only gave Jesus two fish and five loaves was not the point. If he had given only one fish and one loaf Jesus would not have been handicapped. The power was in Jesus, not in the number of fish and loaves.

The measure of my spiritual growth is the extent to which I am willing to give myself and my resources to God. What God does with what I give him is his business.

14 — HOW TO BE A GROWING CHRISTIAN

The questions I am challenged to answer are these: Am I growing spiritually? Am I more aware of God's presence and power in my daily life? Are the qualities of Jesus' personality becoming more and more apparent in my personality? Are more and more of my time, thoughts, talents and treasures being put at the disposal of the people and purposes of God? Or am I becoming more self-centered, more materialistic and more like the society around me? Am I becoming more like the rich man in Luke 12:16-21 or more like the apostle Paul in Philippians 3:7-8?

But all these things that I once thought very worthwhile—now I've thrown them all away so that I can put my trust and hope in Christ alone. Yes, everything else is worthless when compared with the priceless gain of knowing Christ Jesus my Lord. I have put aside all else, counting it worth less than nothing, in order that I can have Christ. (Philippians 3:7-8 Living Bible)

Study Questions

1. In what way is spiritual growth both an event—an experience—and a process?
2. What particular experiences or processes have you gone through which have helped you to grow spiritually?
3. In what sense did Jesus grow spiritually? See Luke 2:52.
4. For the Christian, is spiritual growth an option or an imperative?
5. How has your awareness of God's activity in your life increased recently? What might you do to be even more aware of God's presence in your life?
6. What personality attribute do you need help with? Pray for the Holy Spirit's aid so that you can grow in that area.
7. Are you as available to God as you could be? Have you recently taken steps to make your time, resources, talents and other resources more available to God? If not, how could you?

3
WHY BOTHER?

Why do people go to school? Some people attend school just because the law says they must. But is that why most people go? I don't think so. Most people have a better reason for going. Some go because they have a specific skill they want to learn. Maybe they want to learn to drive a car or a truck. Or maybe they want to acquire the skills of reading and writing, of bookkeeping and computer operation, of retail sales, welding or auto repair. There are lots of reasons to go to school. You can even go to school to become a better parent, to improve your marriage or to learn to fix things around your house.

In a sense, when we commit ourselves to Christ we join a school of discipleship. We don't just enjoy our salvation (although that is important), praise the Lord, and get ready for heaven. Instead, we try to increase our awareness of God, develop spiritual qualities and make ourselves available to God. But why do we try to do all that? I can think of at least three reasons why we should grow spiritually: (1) spiritual growth is *scriptural;* (2) it is *self-fulfilling;* and (3) it gives us *strength* to survive in this world.

It's Natural

It seems to me that God has built the principle of growth right into the universe itself. When God created the fish and animals, he told them to "bring forth . . . according to their kinds," and when he created Adam and Eve he told them to "be fruitful and multiply" (Genesis 1:11-28). He took one man, Abraham, and promised to make his descendants as numerous as the dust of the earth and the stars of heaven (Genesis 13:16; 15:5). Christianity began with one man, Jesus Christ, and grew to twelve, to one hundred twenty, to five thousand and now nearly a billion (Matthew 10:2-5; Acts 1:15; 2:41; 4:4).[2]

Not only do we find the principle of growth in the Scriptures, but there are passages like Ephesians 4:11-16; 1 Thessalonians 3:12, 4:1, 10; and 2 Thessalonians 1:3 where spiritual growth is either commended or encouraged. Perhaps one of the clearest, most direct verses is 2 Peter 3:18 where we are told to "grow in the grace and knowledge of our Lord and Savior Jesus Christ." In 1 Peter 2:2 believers are told to "long for the pure spiritual milk that by it [we] may grow up to salvation."

Of course, Jesus is our supreme example, and Luke 2:52 tells us that he grew mentally, physically, spiritually and socially: "Jesus increased in wisdom and in stature, and in favor with God and man." If Jesus, the Son of God, developed in all these areas, then the mandate for us, his followers, is very clear. We, too, must develop, grow and mature in spirit as well as in body, mind and

WHY BOTHER? **17**

relationships. Spiritual growth is a scriptural principle and a clear biblical command.

Count Your Blessings
Something wonderful happens inside when we look back and see where we've come spiritually. When we take inventory and count our blessings, we might realize that we now have less difficulty loving certain folk, being patient in certain circumstances and exercising faith in God. We realize we have more peace, less confusion and more hope in situations that used to leave us in despair.

When we reflect on our spiritual progress we experience a reassurance and satisfaction. This is not ego-tripping. We know we still have a long way to go, and we recognize that all the progress we have made has been due to God's working in us. But it feels good to be able to look back and see that we have covered some ground toward our goal. Paul expressed it for us in Philippians 3:13-14 when he said:

> No, dear brothers, I am still not all I should be but I am bringing all my energies to bear on this one thing: Forgetting the past and looking forward to what lies ahead, I strain to reach the end of the race and receive the prize for which God is calling us up to heaven because of what Christ Jesus did for us. (Living Bible)

Some unknown bard has expressed the same thing for us in clear language also:

> I'm not what I ought to be
> I'm not what I want to be
> I'm not what I'm going to be
> But thank God
> I'm not what I used to be.

Growing Stronger Every Day
To grow spiritually is to increase in inner strength, stamina and

resilience. To develop spiritual strength is to heighten our possibilities of *survival*.

In Haiti, the mortality rate for children under five years of age is forty per cent.[3] That is very high. But what is the mortality rate of spiritual infants in the average American church? How many persons profess Jesus as their Lord and Savior, join the church, and in six months disappear from the fellowship? Perhaps offering mortality statistics is not the main point of Jesus' parable of the sower (Matthew 13:1-23), but that parable would indicate that seventy-five per cent of the new Christians die before maturity.

Why do infants die? Many die from prenatal diseases and others from complications at birth. But many die because they do not have the strength to overcome the various forces that stand against their survival.

How many infant Christians do we lose because they don't develop the spiritual stamina to survive? In a later chapter I will talk about the "how" of spiritual nurture, but here let's just note that our churches sometimes seem to have revolving doors. As the new Christians come and go, come and go, come and go, they fall by the wayside because they lack the strength to resist the world, the flesh and the devil. It takes strength to make it through the obstacle course posed by Satan, society, the self and the saints. And spiritual growth helps to develop that kind of survival strength (Ephesians 6:10-18).

Growing spiritually also helps give us the strength to face the *struggles* of everyday existence. Life is a constant battle. For some, it is a financial struggle—a fight to make ends meet, to find money for the rent or mortgage, for education, for food and clothes. For others, life is a physical struggle—a fight with diabetes, hypertension, rheumatism or cancer. Life is also a spiritual struggle, a fight with fears and confusion, with doubts and depression, with unresolved relationships and unforgiven hurts and disappointments.

WHY BOTHER? **19**

Often the Lord does not deliver us from these troubles, trials and tribulations. Often he does not deliver us from the fiery furnace of our various struggles because he wants to deliver us *in* the struggles. Sometimes he does not take us out of the fire, but takes the heat out of the flames. In his wisdom, he does not take us out of the lion's den, but takes the ferociousness out of the lion. He did not remove Paul's thorn but gave him sufficient grace to bear it and still be effective (2 Corinthians 12:7-10). In fact, Paul's effectiveness was increased because his weakness displayed God's strength more perfectly.

In spite of our fervent prayers, the Lord does not always remove the thorns from our lives. He leaves them for their educational value. By their presence we learn much about ourselves, about others and about God. Spiritual growth gives us the strength to struggle and in the struggle we develop greater spiritual strength.

Finally, not only does spiritual growth give us strength to survive and struggle, it also gives us strength to *serve*. If we look at the lives of Moses, Deborah, David, Isaiah, Esther, Paul and other people in the Bible, it seems that God is in the habit of giving his people jobs that they can't do—without his help. He never seems to give people jobs that they can do on their own. Did you ever notice that? The Lord always seems to give us jobs that are too big!

Could Moses deliver the children of Israel from Egyptian slavery alone? Would Deborah have known how to defeat the Canaanites without God's help? Could David have overcome Goliath? Could Isaiah carry out his prophetic role? Could Esther save her people from annihilation? Could Paul establish so many churches, write half of the New Testament and develop a Christian theology? No.

Without God's help, could Richard Allen and Charles Mason have established churches for their people? Could Mary Bethune and Booker T. Washington have founded educational institutions? Could Martin Luther King, Jr., have broken down the walls of segregation? No. Not without God's help. Dr. Howard Ferrin, former president of Barrington College, has said that the Lord always gives us jobs that are so big that we need his help to complete them. Without God's help we're sunk!

D. L. Moody, Harold Okenga and Francis Schaeffer were greatly used by God, but they're dead. B. M. Nottage, Benjamin Mays, and Martin Luther King, Jr., were outstanding servants of God, but they're dead. Harriet Tubman, Mary Bethune and Arelia Mallory were effective in their ministries for the Lord, but they're dead. Fanny Crosby, Ira Sankey, and Mahalia Jackson led us in great times of musical praise to God, but they are dead.

We need people today to take the places vacated by these saints of God. There is still much work to be done. Millions of people go to bed hungry each night. This year over four hundred thousand Americans will die from cancer[4] and close to a million from heart-related disorders.[5] There are still millions of alcoholics in our country, and the youth suicide rate is on the increase. The gospel has been preached for almost two thousand years, and yet there are billions of people who have not responded to the love of God in Jesus Christ.[6]

There is work to do. There are big, challenging jobs to be done. And these tasks call for persons of strength. The spiritually weak, anemic and spineless can't do them. But, fortunately, spiritual strength is not something we are just born with. It is not something available only to a select few. Spiritual strength to survive, struggle and serve is available to all who desire it. Are you a Christian? Have you accepted Jesus Christ as your personal Lord and Savior? Then you can be spiritually strong.

Two questions remain: Do I desire spiritual strength? How can I develop the strength necessary to the tasks at hand? Only you can answer the first question. The second question is the one we'll look at next.

Study Questions

1. What is the relationship between Christian survival and spiritual growth?
2. Is it possible to survive as a Christian but not as an effective Christian disciple? Why or why not?
3. Is it possible to have the authority to serve but not the strength to do so? Contrast these episodes in the life of Peter: Matthew 16:19; 26:69-75; Acts 2:14-15.
4. Reflect on the struggles you have faced or are facing. What is the connection between the outcome of your struggles and your level of spiritual strength?
5. While spiritual strength helps you get through struggles, struggles also increase spiritual strength. Explain how this works.
6. Have you ever known someone who made a commitment to Christ and then seemed to fall away from the faith later on? What happened?

4
BUILDING SPIRITUAL MUSCLES

What is it that makes you grow physically? And what prevents good physical growth?

Small babies grow very fast. The average infant will double its birth weight in just a few months. But some infants don't grow as fast. Doctors call this "failure to thrive," and by it they mean that the baby is not growing as quickly as it should. There are many different reasons why this happens.

Some infants are allergic to milk and formula. They do not thrive and grow because they are not receiving the nutrition they need. Other babies never get that food to begin with because their parents are poor and cannot afford the food. Any child who lacks adequate food will not be able to grow as expected.

Other babies do not thrive because they are not stimulated. Have you ever seen on the news a story about a mother or father who didn't know how to raise children and kept them locked in a room most of the time? Such children do not grow properly because they do not have interesting things happening around them. They cannot move around much by themselves, and so their muscles are not developed. No one is with them encouraging them to look at things and to try to do things, so they just lay in their beds doing very little. They do not grow.

Other babies do not grow because they lack love. Around the world there are many children who grow up in orphanages because they have no parents. This happens especially during times of war. During World War 2 studies made on infants in orphanages showed that the children frequently did not grow properly even though they had adequate food and stimulation. What they lacked was love. The orphanage staff people did not have time to pick up and cuddle the babies. Yet without this cuddling some of the children actually died.

In order to grow physically, people need adequate food, good exercise (stimulation) and the right environment (love and encouragement). The same is true for mental growth. People who grow intellectually are those who feed their minds with new information, good literature, art and music, new challenges and new ideas. So why should spiritual growth be any different? It's not.

Right Eating

What is true of physical and mental growth is also true of spiritual growth. There is a certain kind of spiritual diet that nourishes the inner, nonmaterial part of us and causes us to "grow in the grace and knowledge of our Lord and Savior Jesus Christ" (2 Peter 3:18).

Our principal source of nourishment is the Bible, the Word of God. The Bible is a kind of spiritual history of an important part of the human race. It seems that the Lord chose the Jews to be a "for instance," a case study of and for the whole human race. One of the reasons the Bible is so meaningful to so many people is that the things the Jews in the Bible thought, believed and did are typical of all of us. We can see ourselves in each of their successes and failures, their triumphs and tragedies, their assets and their liabilities. They are so much like us and we are so much like them that their journey is our journey and their history is our history.

When we read about Adam's sin, we can understand it: we are faced with similar choices everyday. When Abraham exercises his faith and leaves his home to follow God's leading, we say, "Great!" And when he tells lies under pressure in Egypt, he strikes a sympathetic chord within us (Genesis 12:1-4; 10-20). We feel his struggle as we fill out our income tax forms!

When David wins a victory over Goliath but later sins with Bathsheba, we rejoice with him in his victory and weep with him in his defeat and repentance (1 Samuel 17:1-58; 2 Samuel 11:1—2:23). We have not achieved his victory, nor do we condone his sins, but we have lived awhile, and therefore we understand the Bible as a book that is a reflection of who we are and who we can become.

The Bible is the entrée in our spiritual diet. There are other items on the menu, but the Bible is the main course. Christian books and magazines, informative movies and television programs can all enhance our spiritual growth (if carefully chosen to do so), and time alone, travel and fellowship with other believers also enrich our experience. But all of these are just supplements to the main dish, which is God's Word.

Only in the Bible do we learn who God is and who we are in relation to him. We discover how God is revealed in nature and in history and most perfectly in Jesus Christ. We learn about ourselves and what God wants us to do and be.

In the Bible God speaks clearly and authoritatively. Through his

Word God feeds us his ideals and gives us his warnings, encouragements and praises. In order to grow spiritually, we must read the Bible, study it, meditate on it, live it and share it.

Many books have been written to help us study and understand the Bible as well as possible. We should make use of these tools and set a goal of studying a certain portion of Scripture each day, week or month. We will grow rich in the knowledge of God if we do.

How to Study the Bible by Jack Kuhatschek is a small booklet that will get you started in good Bible-reading habits. *How to Read the Bible* by A. J. Conyers offers practical helps for Bible study. And both these books mention other good volumes to help you delve further. In addition, there are a number of good Bible study guides or monthly Bible-reading programs on the market produced by InterVarsity Press, Nav Press, Walk through the Bible Ministries, and Scripture Union.

Right Exercise

To exercise spiritually means to discover, develop and devote our knowledge, skills and other resources to the glory of God by ministering to people.

The first step in this exercise is *discovering* your assets. Take an inventory of your talents. Has God given you leadership ability? Music or artistic talents? A love for driving? The talent to fix just about anything that's broken? Do you have an inclination toward medicine or law? Teaching or engineering? Counseling or getting to know new people? What are your primary interests? What do you like to do when you can do what you want? What gives you a sense of joy, peace and productivity?

Once you have discovered your talents and interests, then you must *develop* them. Read books and magazines, take classes, go to school and earn a degree if that's necessary to prepare you to use the gifts God has given you. Are you good at fixing things? Then take some courses in electronics, refrigeration and furnace repair and things like that so that you have some technical know-how to match your innate abilities. Do you have the gift of compassion for others? Then look for a degree program in nursing, medical technology or another medical field. But do what you have to do to develop your talents so they can be best used for others.

Then *devote* yourself to using your gifts to serve people and God, your final judge and rewarder. As a Christian, glorifying God is your chief goal in life. And that's the goal you should aim for in using your talents. God didn't give them to you so you could serve yourself, stockpile money and material things, or compete for glory with your fellow human beings. God gave you your particular talents so you could use them for the good of others and for his glory.

As you develop your abilities, you will grow and mature. You may never become a giant in your field, as Beethoven did in music, as Michelangelo did in art, and as Shakespeare did in literature. But that's not what God expects. He expects you to make the most of the talent you have—to do the best you can with your abilities and to use them for the benefit of others. He wants you to grow strong, like a tree planted by a river, whose leaves do not wither but provide fruit for those who pass by (Psalm 1:1-6).

We are not required to be superstars in our fields. We are required to discover and develop our talents, and to devote these God-given abilities and resources to the glory of God and the good of people. We are expected to do and be our best.

> If you can't be a pine on the top of a hill,
> Be a scrub in the valley—but be
> The best little scrub by the side of the rill;
> Be a bush if you can't be a tree. . . .

> If you can't be a highway then just be a trail,
>   If you can't be the sun be a star;
> It isn't by size that you win or you fail—
>   Be the best of whatever you are![7]

Those sentiments may not be expressed directly in the Bible, but certainly Scripture is clear that God wants us to make the most of the talents he's given us.

Yet in addition to developing our skills and using them to serve others, right spiritual exercise means doing what we do with the right attitude—in the right spirit. Moses was not permitted into the Promised Land. God used him to provide the Jews with water out of a rock, but Moses had a wrong attitude (Numbers 20:1-13) and did not follow God's instructions.

Spiritual exercise involves allowing God's Spirit to develop in us a Christlike attitude, an attitude that manifests the fruit of the Spirit (Galatians 5:22-23). Love, joy, peace, patience, kindness, gentleness and the other spiritual fruit are not qualities that are native to us. They are characteristics implanted in our personalities by the Holy Spirit. But they grow within us only with our cooperation.

How does the Spirit put these qualities into us? By strenuous exercise! Frequently the Lord either puts us in situations or permits us to be in situations that stretch us. We may be challenged to love someone who is really obnoxious, to be kind to someone who has taken advantage of us, to forgive someone who has deliberately hurt us again and again, to relate to someone closely who habitually rubs us the wrong way.

These are opportunities for spiritual growth. They are points of interaction with our relatives, friends, colleagues and enemies where the Spirit can make his fruit apparent in us. Through these exercises in love, patience and forgiveness, we stretch, grow, develop and mature.

So it seems there are at least two parts to exercising spiritually: striving to *do* our best in using our God-given talents, skills and abilities; and striving to *be* our best by allowing the Spirit to stretch us and make apparent in us the qualities of Jesus.

Right Environment

What else do we need to grow spiritually? We've seen the need for the right food and exercise. But one more thing is essential. Remember the tree we talked about that grew strong. That tree is described in Psalm 1. The psalm is talking about people who "delight in the Lord," who are faithful and obedient to God. The psalm describes such a person:

> He is like a tree
>   planted by streams of water,
> that yields fruit in its season,
>   and its leaf does not wither.
> In all that he does, he prospers. (v. 3)

This is a wonderful illustration of being in the right environment for growth. What water, sunshine and air are to the tree, good company—both human and divine—is to our spirits.

Samson did not lose his hair, his reputation, his position of leadership and eventually his life because he was a bad person. He was a good brother. He came from a nice home. He was witty, extremely strong and good-looking. The Lord was with him. God chose him to be a leader of his people. But Samson failed because he put himself in the wrong environment. He insisted on marrying a Philistine woman instead of a woman of his own nation. From that point on his dealings with the Philistines began leading him away from God and toward a path of destruction. Finally, another Philistine woman—Delilah—tricked him and he lost all his power (Judges 13—16).

When I was young, my mother used to tell me, "Birds of a feather flock together" and "If you fool with trash, it will get in your eyes." Samson's mother probably told him something like that too. And Paul may have been quoting his mother when he said, "Bad company ruins good morals" (1 Corinthians 15:33). There are not a few young brothers and sisters in prison today because they got mixed up with the wrong crowd. A friend's mother used to say as she came home from work, "Tell me who you've been with, and I'll tell you what you've been doing."

If I want to be a spiritual giant, I can't run with the spiritual midgets. I must stay in the company of spiritual giants or (at least) those who aspire to spiritual maturity. I must stay away from trashy music and magazines. I must be selective in the movies I attend and the TV programs I watch. I must pick my close friends carefully, watch my conversation and guard my behavior.

Above all, I must spend time with Jesus. Ultimately, being spiritually mature means growing to be like Jesus (Ephesians 4:15). He is the model and the real measuring rod of my spiritual growth. John was only a fisherman. But he "hung around" with Jesus and became a theologian and New Testament writer. Matthew was a despised IRS man, but he hung around with Jesus and became a historian. Peter was a hot-tempered, cursing, fighting boatman until Jesus made him a great preacher, writer, evangelist and church leader.

Nobody paid the little group of unlearned people much attention. But they kept hanging around Jesus—listening, asking questions, watching and taking mental notes. And after the resurrection and Pentecost they "turned the world upside down" (Acts 17:6). It pays to hang around with Jesus.

Spend time with Christ in prayer, in the study of Scripture and meditation, in the healing of broken hearts and bodies, in comforting the lonely and distressed, in ministering to the disturbed and downtrodden, in visiting the sick and imprisoned, and in sharing

BUILDING SPIRITUAL MUSCLES 31

the Good News with the lost. And as surely as night follows day, you will become more like Christ.

> Take time to be holy,
> Speak oft with thy Lord,
> Abide in Him always,
> And feed on His word.
>
> Make friends of God's children;
> Help those who are weak;
> Forgetting in nothing
> His blessing to seek.
>
> Take time to be holy,
> The world rushes on;
> Much time spend in secret
> With Jesus alone.
>
> By looking to Jesus,
> Like Him thou shalt be;
> Thy friends in thy conduct
> His likeness shall see.[8]

Study Questions

1. Reflect on the parallels between physical, mental and spiritual growth. What are the basic things needed for growth in each area?
2. What kind of spiritual food have you been eating lately? How might you be able to improve your diet?
3. What spiritual exercises have you done lately? What experiences have tested or stretched you? How did you grow?
4. How can the books we read, the movies we watch or the music we listen to help or hinder our spiritual development?

5. What does it mean to "hang around" with Jesus?
6. Have you been doing much "hanging around with Jesus" lately? How has it helped you to grow?

5
DEVELOPING DAY BY DAY

For some people the Christian life feels like a roller coaster. One day they're up, loving God and obeying him, and the next day they're down, feeling discouraged and distant from the Lord. Or maybe they go to a conference or a revival and hit a mountaintop of spiritual excitement. But then the momentary thrill wears off and nothing in everyday life quite lives up to that mountaintop experience—all seems dull and boring.

God does not want us to live the Christian life that way. His desire is that we will live every day with enthusiasm and consistent faith.

I think there are three key things that can help us to maintain our spiritual development at the very highest level. These are *desire, decision,* and *devotional design.*

A Strong Desire

No one backs into, falls into, or accidentally happens onto a consistently high-level Christian life. No one just wakes up one morning and says, "Wow! This is great. I'm living a strong Christian life!" No. A consistent walk with God is preceded by a strong *desire*. Peter tells his scattered believers in 1 Peter 2:2 that they should "desire the sincere milk of the word" (KJV). David said that his soul longed for God as a thirsty deer pants after water (Psalm 42:1-2). And Jesus said that those who hunger and thirst after righteousness would be filled (Matthew 5:6).

Living a strong Christian life is not natural, easy or automatic. It is first of all the result of an insistent desire by an already committed Christian to live a consistently high-level spiritual life. We must want it and want it badly.

A Definite Decision

Second, in order to keep growing, we need to make a definite decision to do so. It's possible to want something but not make the decision to do what is necessary to obtain it. I have a friend who wants to be "educated." He says that he likes the way educated people think and the opinions they have. Sometimes he even tries to imitate the way some educated people talk and gesture, but he has never decided to go to school to pursue his educational objectives.

The powerful young executive described in Luke 18:18-30 and the other Gospels also needed to make a decision. He desired the kind of life that Jesus had. He probably watched Jesus as he helped blind people to see, lame people to walk and deaf people to hear. He observed Jesus as he forgave people's sins and taught people to love their enemies. This was life at its best, life on a high level, and this rich young executive—I'll call him Richard—wanted it.

So one day Richard made up his mind to have this life, this special Life. (If you read the account in Mark 10:17-27 you can use your imagination to picture it.) After his administrative assistant found out where Jesus was, Richard ordered his chauffeur to drive him to the spot. He could hardly wait to get there. When he arrived, the employees who had come with him were aghast as he jumped out of his Mercedes chariot, ran to where Jesus was, kneeled down in the dust at Jesus' feet and asked breathlessly, "What must I do to inherit eternal life?"

Jesus asked him about the Law, which Richard said he had kept since he was a child. Jesus then looked at him with love and said he would have to sell all of his possessions—his stocks and bonds, his real estate, his businesses, everything—give the money to the poor, and come take up his cross and follow Jesus.

The rich young executive really desired the kind of life that Jesus had, but he couldn't make the decision to pay the cost. Therefore he went away sad. At that moment, he understood more clearly than ever Joshua's challenge: "Choose this day whom you will serve . . . but as for me and my house, we will serve the LORD" (24:15).

Serving God is a tough challenge. And it begins with a decision. Have you made it?

A Devotional Design

Once the decision has been made, the next step in growth is a design. In the last chapter we talked about the need for the right food, exercise and environment for spiritual growth. Knowing that we need those things is good, but we also need a plan to get them.

Daniel was a young man living in a foreign country where the people did not share his faith. Under such adverse conditions it would have been easy to let his spiritual life go to the dogs. But he didn't. He maintained a daily routine of prayer, study and worship. In Daniel 6:1-28 we read that Daniel had a *place*, a *period* and a *pattern* for prayer. His place was beside his window. There he kneeled, with his window opened toward Jerusalem, the city of his heart.

For us the appropriate place is anywhere that we can find peace and quiet to communicate with God. I like to pray in my bedroom. I keep a copy of the *Daily Word, My Utmost for His Highest* by Oswald Chambers, and two or three versions of Scripture beside my bed on a little round table. I like to kneel in prayer, so I also have a small rug that I call my prayer rug. It's not essential to my spiritual life, but it is a tool that helps me to obtain an attitude of reverence and devotion before God.

Different people will have differing styles of communicating with God. The intent is not that we all adopt the same style nor that we all rigidly adhere to a prescribed routine—time of day and length of study. God does not want us to replace one set of commandments with a new set of legalisms. But he wants us to continue constantly to seek him, to study his Word and to communicate with him in prayer. And most of us need a quiet place in which to do that.

Daniel also had a particular period for a devotional time with God. Three times a day he kneeled beside his window to pray. Perhaps the number of times he prayed is not as important as the consistency of his devotional life.

My prayer time is in the morning. That's when I'm freshest, most alert and ready to talk and listen to the Lord. I'm a morning person, so that's my best time of day. In the evening, when some people feel refreshed and ready to go, I'm tired and have been known to fall asleep "before the Lord" as I pray. At that time, unless something is really pressing, I just read the text I'm concentrating on at the time, tell the Lord thank-you for another day, and disappear into slumberland.

Choose the time that's best for you, designate that as your time with the Lord, and meet him every day. Consistency is the key to maintaining your spiritual growth.

In addition to place and period, Daniel also had a devotional pattern. He began with praise. Daniel 6:10 says that Daniel "got down on his knees and prayed, giving thanks to his God, just as he had done before" (NIV). Giving thanks was a habit with Daniel. He knew that he was going to have to face a den of lions, but he didn't weep and wail, moan and groan, complain and send out pity-party invitations. He gave thanks. Much later, Paul would describe this as giving "thanks to God in all circumstances, for this is God's will for you in Christ Jesus" (1 Thessalonians 5:18 NIV).

After Daniel had praised God, he then petitioned God for help. Daniel's pattern reminds us of the devotional pattern Jesus gave to his disciples in Matthew 6:9-13 and Luke 11:1-4. "Hallowed be thy name" always comes before, "Give us this day . . ."

I'm not sure there is ever a time when we should rush into the presence of God begging. Whatever we need to ask for can wait until we say thank-you for blessings already received. Whatever our emergency is, the Lord knew it first and has already made provision for it. The Lord can handle any problem, crisis, dilemma or disaster we experience. And even while we are praying so desperately, he has already taken care of the situation or set the necessary processes in motion. Giving thanks reminds us of that truth, thereby calming our nerves and helping us to quietly and confidently commit ourselves and the whole situation into his hands. How wonderful! "It is good to give thanks to the LORD . . ." (Psalm 92:1).

Could Daniel's devotional design be the secret of his victorious life? Could it be the secret to his ability both to face the lions in the den and the "lions" that put him there? Daniel was not so consistent only because he had nothing else to do but pray. He was a very busy man, a top executive. He was leader over all King Darius's presidents and governors! But he took time to be consistent in his devotional life. As a result Daniel prospered, and God's reputation was proclaimed among all the "people's, nations, and languages that dwell in all the earth" (Daniel 6:25).

Daniel is a wonderful example of a man who maintained a high level of spiritual maturity by having a deep desire for God, by making a definite decision to grow spiritually, and by following a design for his devotional life.

Study Questions

1. Why can't a Christian attain spiritual maturity and strength by accident?
2. In what ways is making a decision crucial to maintaining a high level of spiritual maturity?
3. What is the first decision you need to make on the road to spiritual strength?
4. Why is the rich young executive a good example of a person who had the right desire but made the wrong decision?
5. What were the three parts of Daniel's devotional design? Would you want to add anything to his list?
6. What were the connections between Daniel's devotional life, his political life and his experience in the lion's den?
7. How do daily devotions make a difference in our daily lives—in our relationships at home, work and at church.

6
FAITH FOR THE LONG RUN

The Gospel of Luke contains one of the most beautiful stories in all literature: the story of the Good Samaritan (10:25-37). Jesus told it in response to a lawyer's question, "Who is my neighbor?"

In the story a traveler was attacked and beaten by robbers. They took his money and left him half dead. Two people saw him lying beside the road and they did nothing to help him. But a Samaritan man saw him and gave him first aid and took him to an inn where he could be cared for day and night. This Samaritan man was the true neighbor in the story. The lawyer, listening to the story, recognized that the Samaritan had done the right thing. So Jesus said to the lawyer, "Go and do likewise."

In this pamphlet I have described spiritual growth by concentrating on the three *A*'s: awareness, attributes and availability. By using the three *S*'s—scriptural, self-fulfilling and strengthening—we have thought about the "why" of spiritual maturity. And by considering the three *E*'s—eating, exercise and environment—we have focused on how spiritual growth is encouraged. Finally, I have suggested the three *D*'s—desire, decision and devotional design—as ways to maintain a high-level spiritual life.

Fortunately or unfortunately, spiritual growth does not result from simply reading a book on the subject. In order to get the full benefit, we must follow Jesus' instructions to the lawyer: "Go and do likewise." The discipline of spiritual growth is not easy, but if we accept the challenge we can expect some wonderful rewards.

An Informed Faith

One of the rewards of growing spiritually is a more informed faith. As we draw closer to the Lord and become more like him, we experience greater clarity regarding the what, why and how of our Christian faith. As we consistently study God's Word, pray and worship alone and with others, our own faith becomes more real. What we believe, why we believe it, and how our beliefs have developed to their present state become more transparent. We not only "grow in grace," but also grow in the "knowledge of our Lord and Savior Jesus Christ" (2 Peter 3:18).

Mature Christians do not have all of the answers, but they are able to give a reason for their hope (1 Peter 3:15). A reward for growing up spiritually is a greater ability not only to *live* the faith but also to *express* the faith more intelligently. After being with Jesus for three years, Peter not only stopped cursing but he also became a powerful expresser of the faith (Acts 2:14-36; 3:12-26; 4:8-12).

A Confident Humility

A second reward of spiritual maturity is a more confident humility. To be humble does not mean lying down and letting people walk on you. A proper humility means a correct assessment of your abilities and liabilities. As we read Scripture, we notice two attitudes operating in God's servants. One attitude is bold confidence, and the other is submissive humility.

Moses is a good example. Before God he was very humble. He made all kinds of excuses about his weaknesses, limitations and inabilities (Exodus 3:1-17). But before Pharoah, he stood unflinching and said, "Let my people go!" The reason for such boldness is that Moses knew God would be with him.

Through his Word and our experience, God teaches us that he is awesome in power and strength. We can trust him to do what he says. This gives us tremendous confidence—not in ourselves, but in God and his power. It also makes us very humble because we realize that most of the time he is not working *because of* our abilities but *in spite of* our liabilities. This confident yet humble attitude helps us to go forth and carry out our God-given assignments without getting in the way of our own effectiveness by thinking more highly of ourselves than we ought (Romans 12:3).

A Tender Toughness

A third reward of spiritual maturity is a more sensitive toughness. In *Strength to Love*, Martin Luther King, Jr., spoke of the ideal Christian as being toughminded and tenderhearted.[9] Jesus told his disciples to be wise as serpents and harmless as doves (Matthew 10:16). Another wonderful example of this is found in Luke 19:41-46. There Jesus first weeps over the city of Jerusalem and then drives the moneychangers out of the Temple. In Luke 8:43-48, Jesus is so sensitive that he knows when a sick woman has touched the hem of his robe, but on Good Friday he is so tough that he can stand to be forsaken by God.

It seems to me that one of the things that happens to us as we grow in grace is that we develop the ability to feel more deeply. We develop a greater sensitivity to the hurts, pains, headaches and heartaches of others. And at the same time we develop a toughness to what life does to us. As we grow spiritually, we can take more "stuff," more criticism, more disappointments, more defeats and disasters. We can stand more of these negative experiences without collapsing or taking it out on others.

From the cross, Jesus tenderly cared for his mother *and* forgave his enemies who were crucifying him (John 19:26-27; Luke 23:34). Now that's tenderness and toughness at its ultimate. One of the rewards of spiritual growth is that we grow to be more like Jesus, our model, who is both tender and tough.

A Tearful Joy

Closely related to this tender toughness is the reward of tearful joy. The life of spiritual maturity is not a flowery bed of ease. It is not all peaches and cream. It is not coasting downhill. It is a challenging life, but also a life of joy.

One of the fruit of the Spirit is joy (Galatians 5:22). Jesus told his disciples that he wanted their joy to be full (John 15:11). And Peter declared that the Christian's life of faith is one of "unutterable and exalted joy" (1 Peter 1:8).

Being spiritually mature does not put us beyond trials and temptations, defeats, disappointments and disasters. Problems still come knocking, unfulfilled needs still camp on our doorsteps, unrealized desires still haunt our dreams, and death still snatches our loved ones from us. But for the mature Christian these are stumbling blocks out of which God makes steppingstones. These are some of the "all things" that God works together for our good (Romans 8:28). The Middle-Eastern poet Kahlil Gibran put it beautifully in his book *The Prophet*. He said that the deeper pain carves into our being, the more joy we can contain.[10]

One of the rewards of walking close to Jesus is knowing the fellowship of his suffering and the power and joy of his resurrection (Philippians 3:10; Hebrews 12:2).

Realizing Dreams

A final reward of spiritual maturity is becoming a practical dreamer. Spiritual maturity helps us see the world through spiritual eyes, the eyes of Jesus. Jesus was a visionary, a dreamer of dreams. The focus of his dream was the kingdom of God. He believed that our planet could be free of disease, poverty, crime, war and sin.

So what did he do? He preached, taught and healed the masses. But he also recruited, trained and organized his disciples for world evangelism and discipleship. He sent them out into the world to change it into the image of his dream (Matthew 28:18-20; Mark 16:15-20; Acts 1:8). One of the rewards of spiritual maturity is the sharing of Jesus' vision and the call to work with him to make his dream a reality.

> O Master, let me walk with Thee
> In lowly paths of service free;
> Tell me Thy secret; help me bear
> The strain of toil, the fret of care.
>
> Help me the slow of heart to move
> By some clear, winning word of love;
> Teach me the wayward feet to stay,
> And guide them in the homeward way.
>
> Teach me Thy patience; still with Thee
> In closer, dearer company,

In work that keeps faith sweet and strong,
In trust that triumphs over wrong;

In hope that sends a shining ray
Far down the future's broadening way,
In peace that only Thou canst give,
With Thee, O Master, let me live.[11]

Study Questions
1. What does it mean to be informed about your faith? How would it help you?
2. How can a person be confident and humble at the same time?
3. What is tender toughness? In today's society we hear a lot about being "macho"—strongly masculine and rough. How does Jesus' tender toughness compare to the world's idea of macho males?
4. Describe your idea of the kingdom of God.

Notes

[1] D. B. Norman, *Fourteen Great Thinkers* (Atlanta: Goodpatrick, 1979), pp. 10-12.

[2] Jaroslav J. Pelikan, "Christianity," in *The Encyclopaedia Britannica*, vol. 5 (Chicago: Encyclopaedia Britannica, 1967), p. 693.

[3] According to Bishop Lopez Dautrche of the Church of God in Christ in Haiti.

[4] Alta Rusman, "Cancer Wars," *Pitt Magazine*, University of Pittsburgh Dept. of News and Publication, 1 (September 1986):22.

[5] *Heart Facts*, American Heart Association, 1985.

[6] Pelikan, "Christianity." He estimates the number of Christians in the world as one billion. That leaves approximately three billion non-Christians.

[7] Douglas Malloch, "Be the Best of Whatever You Are," in *The Best Loved Poems of the American People*, ed. Hazel Falleman (Garden City, N.Y.: Garden City Books, 1936), pp. 102-3.

[8] W. D. Longstaff (1822-94).

[9] Martin Luther King, Jr., *Strength to Love* (London: Collins, Fount Paperbacks, 1983), pp. 9-16.

[10] Kahlil Gibran, *The Prophet* (New York: Knopf, 1976), p. 32.

[11] Washington Gladden, 1836-1918.

Further Reading

Barclay, William. *Marching Orders: Daily Readings for Younger People.* Worcester, England: Arthur James, 1973.

Chambers, Oswald. *My Utmost for His Highest.* New York: Dodd, Mead, 1963.

Griffith, Leonard. *Hang on to the Lord's Prayer.* Nashville: Upper Room, 1973.

King, Martin Luther, Jr. *Strength to Love.* New York: Harper, 1963.

Powell, John. *Unconditional Love.* Niles, Ill.: Argus Communications, 1978.

Russell, Daniel. *Meditations for Men.* New York: Abingdon-Cokesbury, 1955.

Thurman, Howard. *Deep Is the Hunger.* New York: Harper, 1951.

——————— . *Disciplines of the Spirit.* New York: Harper, 1963.

——————— . *The Growing Edge.* New York: Harper, 1956.